CANADA'S LAKES & MOUNTAINS

Royce
PUBLICATIONS

(Above) Maligne Lake, Alberta.

Text by Rupert O. Matthews
First published in Canada 1984 by Royce Publications.
© 1984 Illustrations and text: Colour Library Books Ltd.,
    Guildford, Surrey, England.
Display and text filmsetting by Acesetters Ltd.,
    Richmond, Surrey, England.
Printed and bound in Barcelona, Spain.
by JISA-RIEUSSET and EUROBINDER.
ISBN 0 86283 194 6

Sunlight glistens on the ice-capped peaks and sparkles on the rippling waters, for Canada is a land of mountains and of lakes. The towering giants of the Western Cordillera raise their frost-shattered heads above the clouds, while beneath the crests spread azure blue lakes, barely brushed by the breeze.

The greatest of the many thousands of lakes in the nation are surely the Great Lakes of the south. Here some 20,000 cubic kilometres of fresh water swirl and eddy in one of the world's greatest lake systems. Because the lakes are so shallow, compared to their area, the wind can whip the waters into a maelstrom in minutes. Nevertheless, the broad waters are popular with weekend sailors who set out from the great cities of Toronto and Chicago in their pleasure craft. Though they are so well known, the Great Lakes are not the only large sweeps of water in the country. Far to the northwest spread the empty expanses of the Great Bear and Great Slave Lakes. Covering over 60,000 square kilometres between them and plunging to depths of over 2,000 metres, these lakes are among the great features of the Mackenzie District. Supporting fishing industries and with nearby mineral works, they form important transport links during the few weeks of the year that they are free from the terrible grip of the ice.

For sheer numbers of lakes, Canada has no region that can match the ancient Canadian Shield. The low relief and thin soils have made drainage all but impossible over the vast area of land around Hudson Bay. As a result of this, water collects in any hollow and forms shallow lakes that reflect the endless moss-covered landscape, where the caribou feed and the wind howls.

Reflected in the waters of Lake Peyto is a landscape far removed from the tundra of the north. Dramatic, shattered peaks seem to shift and move as the breeze stirs the waters that reflect them. Many of the mountain lakes have a curious milky appearance that adds to their beauty. This beautiful natural phenomenon is the result of tiny rock particles that hang suspended in the water. The mysterious Medicine Lake lies in Alberta. In spring and summer the melting snows fill the lake with up to twenty metres of clear water. The lake then quietly empties, though no stream or river leaves it. The water seeps away through the gravel to join the Maligne River.

The towering, awe-inspiring mountains of Canada are amongst the youngest in the world. Their youth stands revealed in the vigorous upthrust of peaks and the ruggedness of their shapes. Above the tree line the magnificent mountains raise their beautiful, but treacherous heads. The glistening snow and ice turns them into a veritable fairyland of soaring pinnacles and cloud-wrapped beauty. But there is the ever present threat of avalanche, raging blizzard and biting cold. The mountains may be beautiful but their power must be respected. The glories of the Canadian lakes and mountains are, perhaps, the chief beauties of a nation richly endowed with the scenic wonders of nature.

(Previous pages, left) Bowron Lake, B.C.; (right) Millbay, Lake Superior. (This page, above) Howe Sound and (facing page) the Skeena River, B.C.

(Overleaf, left) Red Rock Canyon, Waterton Lakes National Park, Alberta. (Overleaf, right) view from Abbott Ridge, Glacier National Park, B.C.

(Facing page) at Moraine Lake, Alberta, all lies
silent and still within the icy grip of winter's
hand. (Above) Waskesiu River, Saskatchewan.

(Above) a fiery sky colours the waters of Waskesiu
Lake, Prince Albert National Park, Saskatchewan.
(Facing page) tranquil Maligne Lake, Alberta.

(Above) Finger Point, Georgian Bay Islands
National Park. (Facing page) the "Inside Passage"
linking British Columbia and Alaska.

In Alberta lie (overleaf, left) Blakiston Valley,
Waterton Lakes National Park and (overleaf, right)
the Athabasca Glacier, Jasper National Park.

In Kluane National Park, Yukon Territory, lie
Mount Vulcan (facing page) and the Kaskawulsh
Glacier and (above) Slims River.

(Above) a dun, glacier-riven landscape within
Banff National Park and (facing page) Medicine
Lake in Jasper National Park, Alberta.

(Above) placid Bow Lake, Banff National Park,
Alberta. (Facing page) a beaver lodge at the edge
of Amiskowan Lake, Saskatchewan.

(Overleaf, left) mist-shrouded Astotin Lake, Elk
Island National Park, and (overleaf, right)
empurpled Maskinonge Lake, Alberta.

(Above) Western Brook Pond, Gros Morne National
Park, Newfoundland. (Facing page) Mount Harkin and
the mirror-like waters of Kootenay River, B.C.

(Overleaf, left) Tern Island, Kouchibouguac
National Park, New Brunswick. (Overleaf, right)
Prairie Creek, Nahanni National Park, N.W.T.

(Above) Kathleen Lake, Kluane National Park, Yukon Territory. In Banff National Park are found Mount Rundle and Vermilion Lakes (facing page).

Lake Louise (overleaf, left) in Banff National Park, Alberta. (Overleaf, right) Lake Oesa in Yoho National Park, British Columbia.

(Above) sunset comes in shades of gold over a lake in Alberta. (Facing page) the turbulent, foam-flecked waters of Alberta's Athabasca River.

(Overleaf, left) Nahanni National Park, Northwest Territories. (Overleaf, right) golden sunset over Lake Superior.

Astotin Lake, Elk Island National Park, shows its varied moods – from rime-lined shores at dawn (above) to the red shades of sunset (facing page).

(Overleaf, left) twilight approaches at Lillooet Lake, British Columbia. (Overleaf, right) cold, blue meltwater at the Columbia Icefield, Alberta.

Floating images in the waters at Twin Buttes,
Waterton Lakes National Park (above) and (facing
page) Astotin Lake, Elk Island National Park.

(Overleaf, left) Mill Falls in Kejimkujik National
Park, Nova Scotia. (Overleaf, right) Lac en Croix
Brook, La Mauricie National Park, Quebec.

(Facing page and above) scenes along the rugged
coastline of the Pacific Northwest, which is
dominated by the mountain heights.

(Overleaf, left) the shimmering white Columbia
Icefield, Alberta. (Overleaf, right) Muncho Lake,
near the Alaska Highway, in British Columbia.

(Above) pale dawn breaks over Slave River and (facing page) dusk descends at Peace River, Wood Buffalo National Park.

(Overleaf, left) sawmill on the shore of Slocan Lake, and (overleaf, right) Fraser Canyon, between Lillooet and Pavilion, in British Columbia.

(Above and facing page) Medicine Lake, Jasper National Park, Alberta, is a dried-up gravel bed for much of the year, until filled by meltwater.

(Overleaf, left) vista in Prince Albert National Park, Saskatchewan. (Overleaf, right) Peyto Lake, Banff National Park, Alberta.

(Facing page) the town of Waterton Park, Alberta.
(Above) Rogers Pass in Glacier National Park,
British Columbia.

(Above and facing page) snow lies upon the Mount
Odaray Plateau Grand View in Yoho National Park,
British Columbia.

(Facing page) verdant scenery characterises Lake of the Woods. (Above) sunset silhouettes the scene at Astotin Lake, Elk Island National Park.

Glacial Hummock Lake (overleaf, left) in Kluane National Park, and (overleaf, right) Mount Maxwell, in Yukon Territory's Kaskawulsh Ranges.

(Above) the Athabasca Glacier, Columbia Icefield, and (facing page) dipping layered Mount Rundle and the townsite of Banff, Alberta.

(Overleaf, left) Mushroom Peak, Athabasca Valley, Alberta. (Overleaf, right) forked lightning splits the night over Halkett Lake, Saskatchewan.

(These pages) Elk Island National Park, Alberta.
(Above) the sun rising high in its course draws
wraiths of mist from the lake's surface.

(Overleaf, left) St. Lawrence Islands National
Park. (Overleaf, right) the cabin of the writer
Grey Owl, at Ajawaan Lake, Saskatchewan.

(Facing page and above) the Canadian Rockies – a
mountain wilderness where man can still find raw
beauty, and wildlife can find a refuge from man.

(Overleaf, left) scene at Lobster Cove, Gros Morne
National Park, Newfoundland. (Overleaf, right)
Medicine Lake, Jasper National Park, Alberta.

(Facing page) Grose Morne National Park,
Newfoundland. (Above) creek near Shady Lake,
Saskatchewan. (Overleaf) the Rideau Canal.